HIDDEN CODEX OF WEALTH

Uncover the Laws, Break the Programming, and Build Sovereign Wealth

Copyright © 2025 The Codex Bearer

All rights reserved.

ISBN: 979-8-89965-064-2

No part of this publication may be reproduced, stored in a retrieval system, or transmitted in any form or by any means—electronic, mechanical, photocopying, recording, or otherwise—without the prior written permission of the author or publisher. All rights reserved under international and Pan-American copyright conventions.

Legal Notice: This publication is intended for personal use only. You may not modify, distribute, sell, use, quote, or paraphrase any part of this book without explicit consent from the author or publisher.

Disclaimer: The information contained within this book is provided for educational and entertainment purposes only. The author and publisher have made every effort to ensure the accuracy and completeness of the information presented. However, no warranties of any kind are expressed or implied. This book does not constitute legal, financial, medical, or professional advice. Readers should consult qualified professionals before applying any of the information contained herein. By reading this book, the reader agrees that the author and publisher shall not be held liable for any damages, losses, or liabilities caused directly or indirectly by the use or misuse of the information contained in this book, including but not limited to errors, omissions, or inaccuracies.

This book was written in silence, strategy, and lived experience—by one who chose clarity over chaos, ownership over approval, and freedom over permission. May it serve the part of you that's ready to build, not wait.

Table of Contents

Before the Codex 7
   A Note to the One Who Knows Something Is Off 7

PART I — The Constructed Illusion 9
   Chapter 1: The Silent Cage 10
   Chapter 2: The Scarcity Myth 21
   Chapter 3: Who Profits from Your Beliefs? 30

PART II — The Hidden Laws of Wealth 42
   Chapter 4: Wealth Is Frequency 43
   Chapter 5: Rewriting the Inner Code 52
   Chapter 6: The Gatekeeper Principle 62
   Chapter 7: Symbols, Assets, and Power 72

PART III — The Rise of the Sovereign 84
   Chapter 8: Power Habits of Sovereignty 85
   Chapter 9: Creating Wealth Portals 93
   Chapter 10: The Inner Citadel 103
   Chapter 11: The Codex in Practice 114

Before the Codex

A Note to the One Who Knows Something Is Off

You were never meant to feel this trapped.
Not in your work. Not in your finances. Not in your mind.

That quiet ache inside you—the whisper that says *this can't be all there is*—is not confusion. It's memory.
You're remembering that you were born sovereign.

But somewhere along the way, you were given a role instead of a purpose.
You were taught to obey instead of create.
To survive instead of expand.

You were handed a script written by those who profit from your limitation:
Work hard. Take on debt. Buy things. Stay busy.
Don't ask questions. Trust the system. Wait for retirement.
Repeat.

This book is not another success manual. It's not a self-help pep talk.
This is a **codex**—a sacred blueprint—designed to disrupt the illusions that keep you small, broke, and obedient.

It will speak to parts of you that school never reached.
It will challenge beliefs you didn't realize you inherited.
It will equip you with strategies both ancient and modern—
because real freedom requires both consciousness and code.

If you've ever felt like wealth was reserved for someone else...
If you've ever sensed that the game is rigged, but couldn't see

how...

If you know in your bones that you were made for more—
You're not crazy. You're waking up.

And this time, you won't go back to sleep.

Welcome to the Hidden Codex of Wealth.
Let us begin.

PART I — The Constructed Illusion

"To break free, one must first see the cage."

Before you can build real wealth, you need to understand why the system was never designed for your freedom.

You weren't born broken. You were born into a structure—engineered to extract your time, dull your potential, and shape your beliefs to serve someone else's agenda.

This part of the Codex doesn't offer quick wins.
It offers something more powerful: **awareness**.

You'll learn:

- How economic dependence is manufactured
- Why scarcity is a tool of control—not a fact of nature
- Who benefits from your financial disempowerment—and how
- The myths, messages, and systems that keep most people stuck

This is the deconstruction.
The unlearning.
The moment you stop blaming yourself—and start seeing the blueprint that was designed to keep you small.

Because only once you see the cage…
Can you build your way out.

Chapter 1: The Silent Cage

Why the world was never designed for your financial freedom

You were taught that if you work hard, follow the rules, and keep your head down, you'll be rewarded.
That education leads to opportunity. That loyalty leads to security. That success comes from compliance.

But what you weren't told is this:
The rules were designed to keep you predictable, not powerful.
To train you to contribute—without questioning who really benefits.

Chapter 1 is where we expose the structure behind your struggle:

- The system that trains you to trade time for survival
- The educational model built to produce workers, not sovereign creators
- The cultural conditioning that turns comfort into control

This isn't about pessimism. It's about precision.

If you've ever felt like something was off but couldn't name it—
This chapter gives it a name.

Because once you see the design, you stop blaming yourself for outcomes that were never meant to serve you.

You begin the real work:
Not escape—but **reconstruction**.

The Engineered System of Economic Dependence

"If you were free, you would not need their permission to live."

They told you the world was fair.
That if you worked hard, followed the rules, and kept your head down, you'd eventually earn the good life.
But what they didn't tell you is that the rules were written to keep you playing a rigged game.

The modern system you live in was not built to empower you.
It was built to **extract from you**—your time, your attention, your labor, your spirit.
And the most effective extraction method?
An invisible cage you're trained to mistake for freedom.

The Birth of the System: Control by Design

The roots of this cage trace back to the **Industrial Revolution**—a time of machines, mass production, and mechanized labor.
The goal wasn't to cultivate thinkers, creators, or sovereign beings.
It was to manufacture compliant workers who could function in factories, follow commands, and not ask too many questions.

Education systems were restructured to mirror this design:

- Bells to mimic factory shifts
- Memorization over critical thinking
- Obedience over originality

By the time you graduate, you've been trained to trade your time for permission slips:
a job offer, a mortgage approval, a promotion—each one a new leash.

But it doesn't stop there.

The Comfort Conspiracy

Society tells you that this is normal.
You get a paycheck. You buy things to feel alive. You work until you're too tired to question any of it.
This is the **comfort conspiracy**—where just enough dopamine is offered through convenience, entertainment, and short-lived rewards to keep you from revolting.

It's slavery dressed in subscriptions and salary.

The cage is no longer made of bars.
It's made of *numbness*.
And the more comfortable you become, the more asleep you remain.

But there's a deeper price—one few dare to measure.

When you trade curiosity for curriculum…
Imagination for productivity…
Silence for distraction…
You are not just giving up freedom. You are giving up **your essence**.

You were born with a blueprint of purpose—a soul signature designed for expansion, expression, and contribution.
This system doesn't destroy that blueprint. It **buries** it.

Under routines. Under rules. Under the endless pursuit of "enough."

And in its place, you're given an identity not of your own choosing:
A job title. A credit score. A label to wear until you forget you ever had a choice.

This is the true theft.
Not just your time or money—but your **becoming**.

Truth Check-In: Who Owns Your Energy?

Pause.
Look at your calendar. Your bank statements. Your daily thoughts.
Where does your energy go?

If you don't own your attention, your time, or your labor—**you are being rented out**.
Not by force, but by design.

And the most insidious part?
You've likely been taught to thank the system for it.

Activation Exercise: Seeing the Cage

Take out a journal and answer these prompts—no filters, no fluff:

1. **What parts of my life feel like obligations disguised as choices?**
2. **Where do I feel a quiet resistance—but suppress it to stay "secure"?**

3. **If money were not an issue, what would I immediately stop doing?**

These are the bars of your cage.
But awareness turns keys. And keys open doors.

You are not broken.
You are awakening inside a system designed to keep you asleep.

And now, we begin to dismantle it.

The Education–Labor–Debt Trap

From the moment you enter the system, your path is already paved—and it doesn't lead to freedom.
It leads to **predictability**.
To **containment**.
To a life of quiet submission, sold to you as "success."

Let's be clear: education can be beautiful.
To learn languages, discover the cosmos, decipher poetry, understand the laws of nature—this is sacred.
True education ignites the mind, expands culture, and connects us to the depth of human experience.

But the way education is structured carries deep flaws.
While it offers knowledge, it also subtly trains you to fit into a system that does not teach freedom, ownership, or wealth.
It teaches you how to be manageable.

Sit still.
Follow instructions.
Memorize.
Regurgitate.
Perform under pressure.

You're trained not to question the box—but to fight for a better seat *inside* it.

The tests don't measure your potential. They measure your alignment with a predefined script.
And by the time you graduate, the message is etched into your psyche:

"There's a right answer. Someone else has it. Do what they say, and you'll be rewarded."

But the reward is a mirage.

The Conveyor Belt of Modern Slavery

Once you leave school, you're funneled into the next illusion: **the labor-debt cycle**.

College tuition is framed as an "investment"—but the returns are rarely freedom.
You graduate into debt. You chase a job to repay it. You build your lifestyle around that job.
And once you're dependent on that paycheck, your **leverage disappears**.

You are locked into a cycle where:

- You sell your hours to survive.
- You use credit to simulate success.
- You numb your dissatisfaction with consumption.

And society praises you for it.

This is the new assembly line:
Education → Employment → Debt → Consumption → Distraction → Repeat.

And the more exhausted you become, the less likely you are to question it.
Your time is managed. Your creativity is drained. Your rebellion is pacified.

All while the gatekeepers profit off your predictable behavior.

Activation Exercise: Locating Your Programming

Journal on the following with brutal honesty:

1. **What beliefs about money and work were you taught in school—explicitly or implicitly?**
2. **What financial decisions have you made just to "fit in" or look successful?**
3. **If you had been taught how wealth actually works, what path would you have chosen instead?**

Your mind is not broken. It was programmed.

And programming can be rewritten.

Who Profits from Your Limitation

If the system you live in keeps you overworked, underpaid, and spiritually disconnected...
Then ask the real question:

Who benefits from that?

This isn't just a broken system.
It's a perfectly functioning machine—for someone else's profit.

Every time you trade your time for a wage,
Every time you finance your lifestyle with debt,
Every time you internalize the belief that wealth isn't "for people like you,"
Someone wins.

And it's not you.

The Invisible Pyramid

At the top of the economic pyramid sit the gatekeepers—those who benefit not from your empowerment, but from your continued dependence.

Central banks expand the money supply through monetary policy and asset purchases, pumping trillions into the financial system. But this liquidity rarely reaches the people. It fuels asset markets—stocks, real estate, corporate bonds—**enriching those who already own wealth, while eroding the purchasing power of those who don't.**

Corporations build business models on **cheap, expendable labor** and consumers trained to crave convenience over consciousness. They profit when you feel insecure, distracted, and time-starved—because that's when you spend the most, and question the least.

Media conglomerates don't exist to inform—they exist to **shape behavior**. Through repetition, narrative framing, and distraction, they reinforce economic myths: that hard work equals wealth, that the system is fair, and that dissatisfaction is your personal failure, not structural design.

Governments, under the illusion of choice, enforce the conditions of dependency. They subsidize industries that exploit, regulate entrepreneurship into red tape, and offer "relief" that keeps you just functional enough to not revolt. The cycle continues—not by accident, but because it works.

This isn't about conspiracy—it's about **incentive structures**.
The system is not broken.
It functions exactly as it was designed:
To keep wealth circulating in the upper chamber—while the rest compete for crumbs and call it freedom.

They don't need to control you with chains.
They control you with *beliefs*.

You believe you need a degree to be worthy.
You believe you need a job to be safe.
You believe success comes from pleasing authority.

None of this is law. It's just legacy.
Old programming—passed down, reinforced, and never questioned.

Until now.

Manufactured Myths That Keep You Small

Let's name the false doctrines, because they're not just wrong—they're weaponized:

- **"Money is evil."**
  Spoken by people who've never had it—or who want to keep you from claiming it consciously.

- **"Hard work equals wealth."**
  Tell that to the millions grinding 60-hour weeks with nothing to show but debt and burnout.

- **"Success is climbing the ladder."**
  But what if the ladder is leaning against the wrong building?

- **"Rich people are greedy."**
  The truth: money amplifies who you are. The greedy were greedy before the wealth.

Each of these ideas serves a function:
To keep you **energetically repelled** from wealth.
To make you associate money with guilt, shame, or struggle.
To ensure you never become sovereign—because **sovereignty can't be controlled.**

You were never meant to serve systems that shrink you.
You were meant to remember.
And the moment you see the design—you begin to reclaim the blueprint.

Chapter 2: The Scarcity Myth

How artificial lack became the invisible prison

You live in a world of false hunger.
Not because the Earth doesn't provide enough—
but because **scarcity has been manufactured into your mind.**

There is no lack more dangerous than the kind you don't question.
The kind woven into media headlines, casual conversations, government narratives, and economic models.
The kind that whispers: *"There's not enough… so play it safe, settle, compete, obey."*

But here's the truth:

The most valuable resource in the world is not gold, oil, or land—
It's **your belief in scarcity.**

Because when you believe there's "not enough" to go around, you become easy to control.

You become obedient.
You tolerate crumbs.
You view others as competition instead of collaborators.
And you disconnect from your innate ability to create, to circulate, to multiply.

Let's break the illusion.

Scarcity Is Not a Natural Law

Look around.

There is enough food on Earth to feed every human. Enough knowledge to empower every mind. Enough technology to solve global issues at scale.

Yet we still see:

- Massive agricultural surpluses wasted while millions go hungry
- Trillions in wealth extracted from resource-rich nations that remain in poverty
- Markets that would rather **protect profit margins than solve actual need**

This isn't an accident.
It's design.

Scarcity is **profitable.**
It keeps the wheels of fear turning, markets moving, and systems in power.

When people fear they won't have enough, they:

- Work more for less
- Borrow money they can't repay
- Obey systems that promise stability
- Compete with one another instead of questioning the rules

In short: **they become easier to manage.**

Scarcity keeps you locked in survival mode.
And people stuck in survival are too busy scrambling to ever threaten the structure itself.

How Scarcity Is Manufactured Through Media, Policy, and Social Norms

Scarcity isn't just an economic condition—it's a carefully crafted perception.
One that's reinforced so consistently that it becomes invisible.
You don't question it. You adapt to it.
And in doing so, you shrink your vision of what's possible.

You see it everywhere, though you may not realize it:
News headlines that speak of crisis and collapse.
Advertisements that prey on inadequacy and urgency.
Cultural mantras that reward obedience and glorify burnout.

It begins with media.
You're not just receiving information—you're absorbing patterns.
And over time, those patterns shape how you interpret the world, often without your awareness.

Scarcity is broadcast daily: not enough money, not enough jobs, not enough time, not enough safety.
But it's not neutral information—it's a prescription.
The more you internalize it, the more you accept a life of restraint as "mature," "responsible," or "realistic."

And the more you fear there won't be enough, the easier you are to sell to, to manage, to keep in line.

But the illusion goes deeper—into the very policies that govern your life.

You were not taught how money works, how ownership builds freedom, or how to create value from your gifts.
You were shown how to follow directions, manage debt, and chase stability.

Financial literacy was not withheld by accident—it was omitted by design.
Why? Because a population that understands money becomes far harder to control.

Systems of public policy reward dependency while punishing initiative.
Small businesses are buried in red tape while megacorporations are bailed out.
You're taxed for working, but rewarded for borrowing.
And when crisis comes, the solution offered is never liberation—it's sedation.

You're given relief checks, not tools.
You're offered programs, not sovereignty.

And still, the culture around you repeats the script.
Play it safe. Don't be greedy. Be grateful you have anything at all.

So you shrink. You hustle for scraps and call it success. You fear wanting more because no one showed you what it looks like to have more and stay whole.

This is how scarcity becomes a multi-layered illusion—reinforced by every institution and echoed by every norm.

And the deeper it embeds itself, the more it begins to feel like truth.

But it is not truth.
It is a trance.

And every trance can be broken by awareness.

The Difference Between Resource Limitation and Mental Poverty

There's a difference between **having little** and **believing you are little**.

It's easy to confuse external limits with internal worth—especially when you've been taught that success is a reflection of what you possess.
But not all scarcity is physical. Some of it is inherited, invisible, and self-perpetuating.

Resource limitation is real.
Markets fluctuate. Economies shift. Crises happen. Some conditions are genuinely difficult—especially for those born into environments with systemic barriers.

But that's not the full story.
Because two people with the same external conditions can behave in radically different ways—based solely on the **story they carry** about what's possible.

One says, *"This is all I'll ever have."*
The other says, *"This is where I start."*

That's the dividing line between **limitation** and **mental poverty.**

Mental poverty is not just about lacking money.
It's about **living in a state of internalized lack**, where opportunity feels dangerous, expansion feels selfish, and freedom feels undeserved.

It's the difference between:

"I don't have that *yet*" vs. "I'll never have it."
"What's the solution?" vs. "There's no point in trying."

"This is scarce, how can I circulate it wisely?" vs. "There's not enough, so I'll hoard what little I can."

You hesitate to invest, not because it's unwise, but because you don't believe you can recover.
You underprice your work, not because the market demands it, but because your value still feels negotiable.
You delay action, not because it's impractical, but because some voice still says, *"People like you don't do things like that."*

This isn't a mindset flaw.
It's a **mental framework installed by systems that benefit when you play small.**

Scarcity messaging in media, the omission of financial literacy in education, the glorification of hustle without ownership—all of it conditions you to seek safety, not sovereignty.

And if the system can get you to internalize that story, it doesn't have to do much else.
You'll censor your own dreams. You'll reject the very opportunities that could liberate you.
You'll become predictable, manageable, compliant—and call it being "realistic."

This is why more money doesn't always equal more freedom.
If the internal script remains one of fear and unworthiness, the external gain will feel fragile, temporary, or even dangerous.

Real wealth begins when you stop measuring what you have, and start transforming what you believe is possible to create.

You are not defined by your current limitations.
You are defined by your ability to move through them.
And that ability is awakened the moment you stop treating scarcity like a fact—and start seeing it for what it really is:

A filter.
Not a law.

What Ancient Teachings Say About Abundance and Possession

The idea that wealth must be hoarded, defended, or endlessly chased is a relatively modern phenomenon.

In ancient societies, abundance wasn't defined by accumulation—but by access, contribution, and continuity.
People measured wealth not by how much they owned, but by how well they were connected to what mattered—land, community, knowledge, health, tools, and time.

Agricultural traditions understood this clearly.
Planting a seed did not provoke anxiety. The expectation was growth.
The earth was seen as a provider—not a competitor.

Many indigenous and early communal cultures operated on principles of **reciprocity**, not extraction.
If someone had more food, they shared it. If someone had skill, they used it for others.
Status came from what you gave, not what you withheld.

Even ancient trade economies focused on **value exchange** rather than zero-sum gain.
People bartered based on usefulness and mutual benefit—not scarcity-driven pricing.

This wasn't utopia. It had limits, imbalances, and flaws.
But the central point remains: **abundance was seen as something to be cultivated and shared**, not hoarded and feared.

Over time, that shifted.

As economic systems evolved into hierarchies, and possession became a proxy for power, the meaning of wealth changed.

Land was fenced. Labor was commodified. Possession became identity.
And the fear of losing what one had often outweighed the logic of growing or sharing it.

This is where modern scarcity thinking took hold—not from nature, but from structural change.

Ancient teachings remind us of a basic principle:
Access and alignment produce more wealth than anxiety and accumulation.

Whether in Eastern philosophy, early tribal law, or classical political thought, the healthiest systems emphasized balance—between taking and returning, earning and exchanging, consuming and creating.

This isn't about going back in time. It's about remembering that other models of wealth have always existed.
Wealth can be collaborative, not competitive.
Value can be measured by usefulness, not visibility.
And abundance can be pursued **with clarity, not fear.**

Ancient wisdom doesn't ask you to reject modern tools.
It asks you to examine the beliefs you've inherited—and whether they're helping you or holding you back.

Because at its core, the message is simple:

**You were not born into lack.
You were trained to expect it.**

And now, you have the opportunity to choose a different expectation—one rooted in history, reason, and possibility.

Chapter 3: Who Profits from Your Beliefs?

The invisible hands shaping your financial reality

If your life is shaped by the beliefs you carry—
Then the question becomes: *Where did those beliefs come from?*

Most people never ask.
They assume their views on money, success, risk, and value are personal.
But most of those beliefs were planted—by systems designed to shape behavior, direct energy, and maintain control.

This chapter shows you how:

- Financial myths are seeded through culture, education, and media

- Your subconscious was programmed to resist wealth before you could question it

- The system sustains itself by rewarding obedience and punishing sovereignty

You'll also uncover the **false narratives** that keep you energetically repelled from money:
"Money is evil."
"Hard work equals wealth."
"Rich people are greedy."
"Success is selfish."

None of these are truths.
They're tools—used to keep you compliant, small, and disconnected from your own financial potential.

And once you see them clearly, you can choose which ones to keep—
And which ones to burn.

Money Myths That Disempower: "Money Is Evil," "Hard Work Equals Wealth"

Most people don't build their financial beliefs through research or strategy.
They inherit them—passed down from family, media, school, and society until they settle in as *truth*.

And those truths shape how you relate to work, wealth, and even yourself.

The system doesn't need to stop you from building wealth.
It only needs to keep you **mentally allergic** to the actions that would create it.

Let's examine the most common financial beliefs that quietly limit potential—beliefs that feel moral, mature, or realistic, but serve more to preserve hierarchy than to empower people.

- **"Money is evil."**
This idea is rooted in a misused quote. The original line—*"The love of money is the root of all evil"*—warned against greed, not against wealth itself.
But over time, this has mutated into the belief that **wanting money makes you corrupt**.
This belief keeps good people broke. It repels those who could do the most good with wealth from ever pursuing it.
It serves no one—except those who benefit from fewer people competing for power.

- **"Hard work equals wealth."**
This is one of the most persistent myths in modern culture—and one of the most damaging.

Yes, work has value. But hard work alone doesn't explain wealth creation.

If it did, the hardest-working people—nurses, laborers, single parents—would be the wealthiest.

But they're not.

Wealth today is built on:

- Ownership, not just labor
- Leverage (money working for you, not just you working for money)
- Access to information, networks, and scalable value

This myth keeps people stuck in the time-for-money loop, afraid to rest, outsource, or invest.

And it benefits systems that rely on overworked, underpaid contributors who never question the structure.

• "If I just do good work, I'll be rewarded."

This belief promotes passivity. It suggests the world is a meritocracy where effort automatically leads to recognition.

But in reality, people are rewarded for **value delivered, perceived positioning, and communication.**

If you don't advocate for yourself, others will define your worth for you—usually lower than it deserves.

• "Rich people are greedy."

This generalization keeps people at an emotional distance from wealth.

The result? You subconsciously avoid becoming what you've been taught to despise.

But money doesn't create character—it magnifies it.

If you're generous without wealth, you'll likely be generous with it.

If you were ungrounded before success, wealth may exaggerate that.

The solution isn't to avoid wealth—it's to become someone strong enough to wield it well.

- **"Wanting more is selfish."**

This belief is often used to keep people compliant.

It's easier to manage a population that feels guilty for dreaming bigger.

But wanting more isn't selfish when it includes a vision for contribution, service, or upliftment.

More energy, more time, more capital—they allow you to act with purpose, not pressure.

There's nothing noble about struggle for struggle's sake.

Each of these beliefs has been **socialized to sound moral,** but in practice, they create **internal resistance to growth.**

They slow momentum, mute ambition, and keep people fighting to justify why they're staying small.

Because if you believe money is evil,
if you believe success requires endless sacrifice,
if you believe you're only worthy when exhausted—
then you'll never pursue power in a form that frees you.

And that… is exactly the point.

These aren't just thoughts. They're limits, sold as wisdom.
But they can be replaced.

Not with blind optimism. Not with hustle culture.
But with clear, conscious, value-driven strategy.

How Collective Beliefs Are Weaponized to Shape Behavior

No belief exists in isolation.
Your personal thoughts about money, work, and worth aren't just yours—they're part of a larger cultural field.
A **collective operating system** that tells billions of people what's "normal," what's "realistic," and what's "good."

And this field doesn't just influence opinion.
It shapes behavior at scale.

Beliefs become behavior.
Behavior becomes policy.
Policy reinforces belief.

This is how you end up with entire societies that normalize debt, glorify overwork, and quietly shame those who seek freedom.

You're told to work hard—but not to question who profits from your labor.
You're told to save—but not shown how money is devalued while you do.
You're told to give—but warned not to ask for more.

And because everyone around you is operating under the same code, it becomes nearly invisible.

This is how collective myths become **self-policing mechanisms.**

The government doesn't have to tell you to stay in your lane.
Your friends will, your boss will, even your own thoughts will.

You'll call your vision "unrealistic."
You'll fear judgment for stepping outside the narrative.

You'll hesitate not because you're incapable—but because you've internalized the collective rules of the game.

Here's how this plays out in real time:

- **Belief:** "It's risky to start your own thing."
  → **Behavior:** People stay in unfulfilling jobs, suppressing ideas that could have created real value.

- **Belief:** "Talking about money is rude or arrogant."
  → **Behavior:** Financial illiteracy remains high, and money shame stays unspoken.

- **Belief:** "Be grateful for what you have."
  → **Behavior:** People stay stuck in survival mode, calling stagnation a virtue.

These beliefs aren't accidental.
They function as **behavioral scripts**—rewarding conformity, punishing deviation, and maintaining stability for those at the top.

When a belief becomes widespread, it no longer feels like a suggestion.
It feels like *reality*.

This is why changing your financial life isn't just about learning new strategies.
It's about **unlearning collective obedience.**

You're not just escaping old habits.
You're stepping outside the story that shaped them.

And the moment you do, you'll see something powerful:

Most people aren't failing.
They're just following.

First Exercises to Begin Mental Deconstruction

Breaking free from financial programming doesn't start with a spreadsheet.
It starts with awareness.

Before you can rebuild your beliefs around wealth, you need to dismantle the ones you didn't choose—but have been living by.

This is not about guilt or blame.
It's about clarity.

These exercises are designed to help you spot the inherited scripts running quietly in the background—so you can start choosing your beliefs on purpose.

Set aside 15–30 minutes.
Be honest. Be specific. Don't filter.

Exercise 1: Spot the Source

List three beliefs you hold about money, wealth, or rich people.

Now for each, ask:

- Where did I first hear this?
- Who in my life modeled this belief?
- What did that belief teach me to fear or avoid?

The goal is not to judge the belief—just to **trace its origin**.

Exercise 2: Challenge the "Truth"

Choose one of your core financial beliefs and ask:

- Has this belief consistently helped me grow, build, or feel empowered?
- Who benefits when I believe this?
- What if the opposite were true?

Sometimes the belief isn't wrong—but it's **incomplete**. This exercise helps you fill in what's missing.

Exercise 3: Rewrite the Script

Now take a belief you want to change and reframe it into a new mental default.

Old belief: "Money is hard to come by."
New belief: "Value is created—and I know how to create it."

Old belief: "I have to work harder to earn more."
New belief: "I get paid for value, not hours."

Old belief: "Wanting more is selfish."
New belief: "Having more allows me to do more—for myself and others."

Write your new belief clearly. Then write **one small action** you can take this week to embody it.

Now actually do it.
Don't wait for the perfect time. Don't overthink it.
The shift begins the moment you act—not perfectly, but *deliberately*.

One step taken from a new belief carries more power than a hundred intentions from the old one.

Change doesn't come from force—it comes from **frequency.**

The more often you challenge your old code, the faster your new one takes hold.

You don't need to solve everything overnight.
You just need to start seeing clearly—and choosing consciously.

That's how deconstruction becomes power.
That's how a belief system becomes yours.

PART II — The Hidden Laws of Wealth

"What you see is not all that is. True wealth begins in the unseen."

You've broken the illusion.
Now it's time to build the reality.

If Part I revealed the cage—
Part II gives you the keys.

This is where you learn to work with **unseen architecture**:
The laws beneath the surface. The energies behind action. The patterns that govern real wealth—not just in theory, but in practice.

Because wealth isn't just about strategies. It's about **alignment**. It's about resonance, awareness, and the ability to act in sync with what actually creates value and flow.

The people you admire, the ones who seem to "attract" success—they're not lucky.
They're attuned.

They operate on different assumptions, respond to different signals, and **play a different game entirely.**

Now, so will you.

Chapter 4: Wealth Is Frequency

Money as Energy, Focus, and Resonance

You've been taught that money is a thing.
A number in a bank account. A piece of paper. A goal on a vision board.

But money is not a thing.
It's a **signal.** A **frequency.** A measurable result of how value is created, perceived, and moved.

Wealth, in its most accurate form, is a form of **resonance**—an alignment between internal state, external action, and collective value.

This is why two people can apply the same strategy, read the same books, and take similar steps—yet only one of them breaks through.
It's not just about action. It's about **who they are when they act.**

Money is not chasing effort.
It's responding to **alignment**—of belief, energy, clarity, and execution.

You are not just an economic actor. You are a broadcasting system.

Every thought, belief, habit, and decision you make emits a frequency.
And wealth responds—not to what you *want*, but to what you're *tuned to*.

Manifestation Redefined: Energy + Clarity + Aligned Action

You've probably heard the word "manifestation" tossed around.
Visualize. Speak it into existence. Think positively.
It sounds appealing—until you try it and nothing happens.

Because manifestation isn't about wishful thinking.
It's about alignment between **internal frequency** and **external behavior.**

☑ **Desire without action is fantasy.**
☑ **Mindset without movement is inertia.**
☑ **Manifestation is real—but it only works when it's grounded in energy, clarity, and aligned action.**

Let's break that down:

Energy is your baseline emotional and mental state.
It's what you project without trying. It's the invisible signal you carry into every room, every conversation, every decision.

If your energy is wired to fear, lack, and self-doubt, it doesn't matter how much you "want" wealth—your actions will subconsciously avoid it.

Energy sets the tone.

Clarity is the target.
What exactly are you building? Why does it matter?
Clarity creates precision—and precision reduces resistance.

Most people fail to attract or build wealth because they're vague.
They say they want more money—but they haven't defined the **form,** the **function,** or the **purpose** of that money.

The universe doesn't respond to confusion. Neither do markets.

Aligned Action is the bridge.
This is where manifestation becomes material.

You don't just sit and visualize.
You take steps, make moves, solve problems, show up consistently—with decisions that reinforce your frequency and your focus.

And here's the key: your action has to match your intention.

You can't say "I want financial freedom" and continue to say yes to every job that drains you.
You can't say "I'm a creator of value" and spend your time avoiding the work that would prove it.

Alignment means your **choices support your claim.**

Manifestation isn't magical thinking.
It's a system—one that works when your energy, your vision, and your behavior are operating in sync.

When people say, "it just started flowing," what they're really describing is **resonance**.
Their internal state finally matched the outcomes they were ready to receive.

And when that happens, effort becomes effective.
Opportunities feel drawn to you—not because you're lucky, but because you're *clear*.

How Your Financial Results Mirror Your Energetic Set Point

Wealth doesn't respond to what you want.
It responds to what you *expect*.
And those expectations are shaped not by positive thinking—but by your **energetic baseline.**

Everyone has a set point—a default internal setting around how much ease, freedom, and abundance they allow into their life.
It's not what you consciously affirm. It's what your nervous system is calibrated to handle.

If you've been taught that struggle is normal, you will unconsciously recreate it.
If you believe deep down that earning money must feel hard, you'll ignore or reject paths that feel easeful.
If you've associated wealth with danger, judgment, or isolation, you'll sabotage it the moment it begins to grow.

This isn't weakness—it's programming.

You don't attract what you fantasize about.
You attract what you are energetically *available* for.

And availability is trained.

This shows up in subtle ways:

- You procrastinate making an offer, even though you know it would serve people.

- You underprice your work, not because of market research, but because part of you doesn't believe you're worth more.

- You invest time, but hesitate to invest money—because safety feels more familiar than expansion.

This is how your **inner thermostat** governs your results.
Even if you double your efforts, you'll unconsciously adjust your behavior to stay within the range that feels "safe."

This is why some people plateau at certain income levels—even when they have more knowledge or skill than those earning ten times more.

Their set point hasn't shifted.
And until it does, their results won't either.

But here's the opportunity:

Your set point is not fixed.
It's a reflection of your emotional conditioning—and emotional conditioning can be rewired.

Just like a muscle, it responds to challenge and repetition.

When you act from a higher standard—even before you fully believe in it—you begin to raise the baseline.
You normalize bigger numbers.
You grow comfortable with greater visibility.
You expand your capacity to hold success without panic or sabotage.

This is the inner work that magnifies outer results.

It's not glamorous.
It's often invisible.
But it's the foundation that determines whether your strategy succeeds or stalls.

Because you don't rise to the level of your vision.
You rise—or fall—to the level of your energetic set point.

The Law of Resonance and How the Wealthy "Tune" Themselves to Attract

The wealthy don't just work differently.
They *think*, *move*, and *respond* from a different internal frequency.

This isn't about superiority.
It's about **resonance**—the principle that what you consistently *are* becomes what you consistently *attract*.

Resonance isn't magic. It's mechanics.

In physics, when two frequencies align, they amplify one another.
In human behavior, the same is true.
When your internal state is coherent—clear, focused, stable—you become a magnet for opportunities, people, and resources that match that signal.

Wealth responds to this kind of alignment.
Not just because you "deserve it," but because your field becomes **congruent** with what you're asking for.

Here's how the wealthy tune themselves:

- **They protect their attention.**
  Because they know attention is energy—and energy spent in distraction is opportunity lost.

- **They normalize bigger numbers.**
  What scares others is familiar to them. They've trained their nervous system to hold scale without collapse.

- **They operate from vision, not reaction.**
  They don't wait to feel ready. They move in alignment with what they've committed to becoming.

- **They surround themselves with aligned energy.**
  Environments matter. Conversations matter. Input equals output.

None of this is about luck or "high vibes."
It's about **deliberate attunement**—shaping your mental, emotional, and behavioral patterns to reflect the outcomes you're aiming to create.

Most people wait for circumstances to change before they change their state.
But that's not how resonance works.

Resonance means *you shift first*.
And then, reality recalibrates around that shift.

This is why the same tactic, offer, or business model works for one person and fails for another.
Because what matters most is *who* is running it—and what frequency they're running it from.

When your external strategy is aligned with an internal frequency of ownership, trust, and direction—results come faster.
Not because the world changed, but because you did.

And that's the hidden law:
Wealth isn't pursued. It's aligned with.
And alignment begins inside.

Chapter 5: Rewriting the Inner Code

Destroying poverty programming and installing wealth identity

---

You can't build wealth with a mind that's wired for survival.
You can try—grind harder, hustle smarter—but the results will always be limited.

Because beneath every strategy is a system.
And beneath every system is a self-concept.

If you've been programmed to believe that struggle is noble, money is dangerous, or success isn't for people like you, then every opportunity will feel unsafe.
Every breakthrough will trigger sabotage.
And every win will feel like an accident instead of alignment.

Wealth is not just what you earn.
It's what you can *hold*.
And what you can hold is determined by your **identity.**

That identity—the internal code that governs your expectations, decisions, and sense of possibility—is not fixed.
It can be rewritten.

And that's what this chapter is about.

How Subconscious Imprints Sabotage Abundance

Most people never question why they self-sabotage.
Why they hesitate right before the breakthrough.
Why they lower their price at the last minute.
Why they delay the launch, ghost the opportunity, or downplay the win.

They think it's fear, laziness, or bad timing.
But it's not.

It's code.

Deep in your subconscious, long before logic kicks in, you've been programmed with beliefs—imprints—that define what is *safe* to receive, express, and pursue.

These imprints don't just shape your thinking.
They govern your behavior.
They override your intentions.
They act like a firewall—blocking anything that threatens the status quo of your inner identity.

Where do these imprints come from?

- **Family dynamics:**
  What did your caregivers model about money, success, and self-worth?
  Was money a source of stress? Were wealthy people criticized or admired? Was ambition encouraged or shamed?

- **Cultural norms:**
  What were you taught growing up about "what people like us do"?

Were certain careers seen as respectable while others were off-limits?

Did your environment equate wealth with corruption—or with freedom?

- **Early experiences:**
  Your first financial memories matter.
  Getting shamed for asking for too much. Being rewarded for staying quiet. Watching someone succeed and then lose everything.
  These moments imprint not just ideas—but *emotional triggers* that stay encoded until addressed.

These subconscious blueprints become your **default operating system.**

Even when you "know better," you'll find yourself repeating the same patterns—because your nervous system hasn't caught up with your vision.

This is how it shows up:

- You create a brilliant offer—then unconsciously price it low to avoid judgment.

- You get unexpected income—then spend it fast because holding it feels uncomfortable.

- You dream of expansion—but keep choosing safe, low-leverage paths that don't challenge your identity.

It's not because you're weak or broken.
It's because you haven't updated the software.

To step into wealth, your subconscious needs to see it as **safe, normal, and aligned.**

Not foreign. Not dangerous. Not forbidden.

This isn't just mindset work. It's **identity repair.**

Because until your inner code matches your outer goal,

You won't grow—you'll loop.
You won't expand—you'll resist.
You won't rise—you'll retreat.

But once you see the code, you can change it.

And that changes *everything*.

Mental Filtering: Why Poor Mindset = Blind to Opportunity

Opportunities aren't always obvious.
In fact, they're often subtle—disguised as effort, hidden in unfamiliar language, or wrapped in risk.

This is why two people can look at the exact same situation…
and only one sees potential.
The other sees threat, confusion, or "not for me."

The difference isn't intelligence or talent.
It's **filtering**.

Your mind doesn't process every piece of information equally.
It filters based on what feels *relevant*, *safe*, and *possible*.
And those filters are shaped by belief.

If your internal code says "wealth is for other people," then when opportunity shows up, your brain won't even register it as real.
You'll scroll past it. Dismiss it. Rationalize it away.
Not because it's not valid—but because it doesn't fit your mental model of what's available to you.

This is the silent cost of poverty mindset:

- You don't apply for the funding because you assume it's not for someone like you.

- You undercharge your service because you believe the market won't pay more.

- You pass on a powerful collaboration because it feels "out of your league."

- You waste hours looking for free solutions instead of investing in acceleration.

And each time you do, your subconscious gets reinforced:

"See? Wealth isn't for me. I don't have access."

But it's not access you lack.
It's alignment.

Opportunity is often already present.
But until your internal filters change, you simply can't see it clearly enough to act on it.

The mind protects its beliefs—even at your expense.

This is why many people sabotage growth.
It's not that they fear failure—it's that success threatens the story they've lived in.

If you suddenly become visible, what happens to your identity as the underdog?
If money comes easily, who are you without the struggle?
If abundance is normal, what excuses disappear?

Growth demands a new frame.
One where success is not exceptional—it's *expected*.
One where possibility is not the exception—it's the baseline.

This doesn't mean you see opportunity everywhere overnight.
But it does mean you start asking different questions.
Instead of: *"Why would this work for me?"*
You begin to ask: *"What would it take for this to work?"*

That single shift in framing can change everything.

Because clarity doesn't come from outside.
It's something you train your mind to detect.

Practices: Inner Coding, Affirmations, Rewriting Your Money Story

Awareness opens the door.
But **repetition rewires the system.**

You can't reprogram decades of financial conditioning with a single insight.
You need new inputs—spoken, written, and embodied—fed into your nervous system until they become the new baseline.

This isn't about "thinking positive."
It's about deliberately reshaping your **inner narrative**—so your identity, your behavior, and your results begin to match.

Let's get practical.

---

1. Inner Coding: Install a New Identity

Start with a simple but powerful question:

Who am I when I operate from wealth, not lack?

Let your answer be bold, specific, and embodied. Don't describe what you have—describe **how you show up.**

Examples:

- I take decisive action instead of waiting for permission.
- I make offers, set boundaries, and invest with clarity.
- I speak about money without shrinking or apologizing.
- I no longer confuse humility with playing small.

Write a list of 5–10 identity traits. These become your **inner operating instructions.**

Reread them daily. Speak them aloud. Step into them when you make decisions.

2. Affirmations that Resonate (Not Just Sound Good)

Affirmations only work when they're close enough to be **believable**, but bold enough to feel **expansive.**

Don't lie to yourself. Stretch yourself.

Examples:

- "I'm learning to hold more wealth with calm and clarity."
- "Every day, I act more like someone who is financially free."
- "I no longer chase money—I build systems that attract it."
- "I trust myself to make powerful financial decisions."

Write 3–5 of your own. Then anchor them into daily life:
Say them before sending an invoice, making a sales call, opening your banking app.
Connect the words to action.

3. Rewrite Your Money Story

Journal on this prompt:

What is the old story I've been living around money, and what is the new story I now choose to live?

Example:

- **Old Story:** I have to work harder than everyone else to deserve enough.
- **New Story:** I create value intelligently. I earn with precision, not exhaustion.
- **Old Story:** Money always comes and goes. I can't hold it.
- **New Story:** I'm a capable steward of wealth. I manage, multiply, and protect my resources with skill.

Write yours down. Read it every morning for 30 days. If new beliefs or insights come through during that time, write them down and integrate them. Your story is allowed to evolve—just like you.

Each time you take action aligned with your new story, you reinforce the code.

This is how internal change becomes external result:
Not overnight. Not by magic.
But through **deliberate reinforcement of a new identity— until the old one no longer runs the show.**

You don't need to be perfect.
You just need to be consistent.

Repetition creates rhythm.
And rhythm creates reality.

Chapter 6: The Gatekeeper Principle

How the elite use systems of control to stay rich

Wealth is not just accumulated—it's **protected, gated, and multiplied** through systems.

While most people are taught to focus on hard work and personal finance, the wealthy operate through **access, information, and flow.**

And the biggest secret?

The rules are different depending on which side of the gate you stand.

The system was never designed for equal participation. It was built to reward those who understand how to move capital, manage risk, and shape perception—while keeping everyone else focused on survival, scarcity, and savings accounts.

This chapter isn't about envy.
It's about **architecture.**
If you don't understand the structure, you can't play the game. And if you don't know how the gatekeepers operate, you'll spend your life waiting for permission that was never meant to come.

It's time to decode how the top stays at the top—and how you can step beyond the gate.

Access, Leverage, and the Manipulation of Flow

The wealthy don't get rich by trading time for money.
They get rich by **controlling flow**—of capital, attention, information, and opportunity.

At the center of that control are three forces:
Access. Leverage. Flow.
Once you understand these, the illusion of equality disappears—and strategy becomes clear.

---

1. Access: The Hidden Layer of Wealth

Most people are taught to focus on *what* they know.
The elite focus on *who* they know—and more importantly, who knows them.

Access is the difference between:

- Getting funded or being ignored
- Hearing about a deal before it's public
- Solving a problem with one phone call versus five years of trial and error

This isn't just about privilege—it's about **proximity to flow.**
Flow moves through relationships. Closed rooms. Trusted networks.
And if you're not in the room, it doesn't matter how smart or capable you are—you don't exist in that economy.

The good news? Access can be built.
But it requires intention. You need to add value, show up strategically, and think in decades—not just days.

2. Leverage: The Wealth Multiplier

The wealthy rarely earn through effort alone.
They use leverage: **tools that allow results to compound without matching increases in time.**

Types of leverage:

- **Capital leverage:** Using money to make more money—through investments, equity, or interest.
  This is how the wealthy multiply while resting: their assets work even when they don't.

- **Media leverage:** One message seen by thousands, or even millions, while you sleep.
  A single message—when delivered through the right platform—can generate reach, trust, and income without constant repetition.

- **Technology leverage:** Systems that run without you—landing pages, automations, scalable delivery.
  It allows a few days of smart building to keep delivering value long after you've stepped away.

- **Team leverage:** Hiring people whose skills, time, or perspective extend your reach.
  You can't buy more hours—but you can borrow other people's genius.

Leverage is how one person can create the results of a hundred. It's not unethical. It's intelligent.

What's unethical is teaching people that *harder work* is the only path—while you quietly scale through smarter systems.

3. Flow: The Currency Beneath Currency

Money is not static. It moves.

And the wealthiest people aren't chasing money—they're positioning themselves where **money already flows.**

They know:

- Where capital is moving next
- Where attention is gathering
- Where market narratives are shifting

And they position themselves there **before the crowd arrives.**

They don't need to gamble.
They understand the game board.

This is what keeps the gates closed to the average person:
Not lack of work ethic, but lack of **pattern recognition.**

The system doesn't hide this information.
It just makes sure you're too distracted, overworked, or under-resourced to study it.

But once you see it, you can stop playing the game of effort—
and start building systems of leverage and alignment.

Because wealth is not about hoarding.
It's about **flowing in the right direction—at the right level—with the right tools.**

Attention Arbitrage Explained Clearly

In today's economy, **attention is currency.**

And just like any currency, it can be captured, exchanged, or multiplied—if you know how.

The elite understand this.
They don't just sell products or ideas.
They **leverage the platforms**, shape the narratives, and position themselves where **attention naturally concentrates.**

But what does it mean to leverage a platform?

It means using a system you don't own—strategically and intentionally—to multiply your outcomes.

You don't own Instagram, but you can build a business off its reach.
You don't own YouTube, but one well-placed video can generate leads for years.
You don't own a podcast network, but a single high-trust interview can open doors for a lifetime.

You're not building the machine—you're using it with precision. And the elite understand where people are looking—then place themselves there, consistently, *before* everyone else.

This is called **attention arbitrage**—and it's one of the most powerful, misunderstood forces in modern wealth creation.

What is attention arbitrage?

Arbitrage means profiting from a gap—buying something at one price and selling it at a higher one elsewhere.

Attention arbitrage means capturing attention where it's cheap or underutilized—and redirecting it toward outcomes that convert at a much higher value.

Examples:

- Turning organic content (free attention) into high-ticket offers (high return)
- Building a personal brand that drives trust, which lowers acquisition costs
- Taking underpriced attention on one platform (e.g., TikTok) and funneling it into owned assets (email list, product, community)

It's not about manipulation.
It's about **intelligent placement**.

If you know where people are looking—and what they're missing—you can position yourself as the bridge.
And bridges get paid.

Why does this matter?

Because the traditional economy says: work hard, be consistent, and hope someone notices.

But in reality, the winners are the ones who:

- Know **where attention is undervalued**
- Build assets that capture it efficiently
- Turn attention into trust—and trust into revenue

Most people are consuming attention.
The wealthy are converting it.

Examples of how this shows up:

- A creator offers massive free value on a podcast, then converts a percentage of loyal listeners into high-trust clients.

- A startup invests early in an overlooked ad platform and dominates a niche before competitors arrive.

- A thought leader uses viral ideas not to go "viral," but to drive traffic to long-term assets like books, courses, or platforms.

In every case, the game isn't just content.
It's **conversion through intelligent positioning.**

The takeaway isn't to become an influencer or marketer.
It's to realize that **if you're invisible, you're at the mercy of others.**

And the moment you learn how to channel attention toward aligned value—you stop chasing.
You start attracting.

Because in the modern world, **the one who owns attention owns leverage.**

Social Networks, Deal Flow, and Insider Strategy Decoded

There's a reason the wealthiest people often seem to play by different rules.
It's not just mindset. It's **placement**—inside ecosystems that most people never even see.

These ecosystems run on three currencies:
Relationships, reputation, and relevance.

And when you're in the right circle, wealth doesn't just grow—it compounds.

This isn't about elitism. It's about **flow.**
Because money moves fastest through trust. And trust is relational.

What is deal flow—and why does it matter?

Deal flow is the steady stream of investment opportunities, partnerships, and insider information that circulates behind closed doors.

If you've ever wondered how certain people get in early on the next big thing—this is why.
They're not guessing.
They're being shown.

When you're inside the right network:

- You hear about business opportunities before they go public
- You get invited into private deals, collaborations, and capital circles

- People bring you leverage—because you're known, trusted, and visible

Most people think success is about having the best idea.
But in reality, it's about having the right **network to move that idea through.**

Why most never access it:

Because the gatekeepers don't advertise.

You won't find "deal flow" on a job board.
You won't get invited to pitch in a random DM.

Access is based on **proximity and proof:**

- Who vouches for you?
- What do you bring to the table?
- Do you operate with integrity, precision, and long-term thinking?

And most importantly:
Do you move like someone who's already in the flow?

That's the paradox:

You often have to embody insider energy—*before* you're fully inside.

How to position yourself strategically:

You don't need to fake status or force connections.
You need to **become visible in the rooms that matter—by providing value that matters.**

Start with:

- Showing up where your ideal peers, mentors, or collaborators already are
- Publishing thought leadership that positions you as a builder, not a beggar
- Offering value first—without expectation
- Playing the long game: trust compounds faster than likes or hype

This isn't overnight.
But over time, your **reputation becomes your referral system.**
And when the right people know you're serious, you get pulled into opportunities you'd never reach on your own.

In the hidden economy, it's not just *what* you know—or even *who* you know.
It's who knows **you**—and what they associate with your name.

That's not ego.
That's architecture.

And once you're in the flow, the game changes.

You stop knocking.
You start getting invited.

Chapter 7: Symbols, Assets, and Power

What the rich actually value—and why

Wealth isn't just money.
It's **stored influence.**
It's value crystallized into forms that grow, protect, or command attention over time.

That's why the rich don't just chase cash.
They collect **symbols.**
They build **assets.**
They move with an understanding of **power**—not as dominance, but as positioning.

They think in terms of:

- Ownership, not wages
- Multiplication, not accumulation
- Presence, not just performance

This chapter reveals how the elite define value differently—so you can begin doing the same.

Because once you see how they store power, you can stop consuming like a worker and start building like a sovereign.

Why Wealthy People Buy Equity, Not Expense

Wealthy people don't just spend money.
They **position it.**
And what they position it into isn't consumption—it's **control.**

The middle class is taught to show success by spending:
New car. Bigger house. Branded lifestyle.

The wealthy show success by **owning the thing that makes the money.**
That's called **equity**—and it's the core financial language of the rich.

What is equity, really?

Equity means ownership in something that has the potential to grow in value or produce returns.
It could be:

- A share of a business
- Real estate that produces income
- Intellectual property (books, patents, courses)
- Brand equity in your own name or company

Equity produces **leverage**.
Instead of earning once, you earn continuously.
Instead of working for money, money works for you—because you own a percentage of the upside.

Expenses vs. Assets: A Different Lens

When most people get a windfall, they ask, *"What can I buy?"*
The wealthy ask, *"What can I own that pays me later?"*

This mindset shift creates dramatically different outcomes.

- **Buying a luxury car?** For most, it's a depreciating expense.
  The value drops the moment you drive it. It doesn't produce cash flow or equity.
  However, rare collector cars—like vintage Ferraris or limited editions—can appreciate over time *if* kept in pristine condition.
  In that case, the purchase may act as a strategic asset, similar to art or rare collectibles.
  But for the average buyer, it's still a liability—not a wealth builder.

- **Buying a rental property that pays monthly cash flow?** That's an income-producing equity play.
  You own something that continues to pay you—whether you're working or not.

- **Buying designer clothes?** Expense.
  You wear them once, post the photo, they sit in the closet.

- **Building a personal brand with strategic media assets?** Equity.
  You become a magnet for speaking, deals, and business opportunities.

The wealthy aren't anti-luxury.
They just **earn from the asset first—then buy the luxury from the yield.**

They don't sacrifice enjoyment.
They **sequence** it.

Why this matters:

Equity compounds.
Expenses decay.

And if all your income goes toward things that lose value the moment you buy them, you'll never escape the earning treadmill.

How to Shift Toward Equity Thinking

This isn't about cutting all pleasure or becoming a financial monk.
It's about **training yourself to prioritize ownership before indulgence.**

Start here:

- When you want to spend $500 on something, pause and ask: *Can I put this toward something that will pay me later?*
- Before buying a non-essential item, challenge yourself to invest an equal amount in something that builds value
- When you get a windfall, don't just reward yourself—**reposition part of it** into equity: a skill, an asset, or a system

This small pattern shift rewires your relationship to money.
You stop consuming to feel better—and start investing to become stronger.

True wealth isn't in what you buy.
It's in what keeps paying you—whether you show up or not.

That's why equity is the language of freedom.
It's what separates income from effort.
And it's the foundation of how sovereigns build power.

Symbols of Power: Ownership, Brand, Reputation

Not all wealth is visible.
But some of the most powerful forms of wealth are designed to be seen—not as ego displays, but as **symbols of authority, positioning, and influence.**

These are the **social signals** that indicate status—not just in terms of money, but in terms of **power, trust, and sovereignty.**

And the most strategic among the wealthy use these symbols not to impress…
But to **negotiate, attract, and amplify.**

Let's break them down.

---

1. Ownership

This is the foundational symbol of power.
To own is to control—and control creates freedom.

Ownership could mean:

- Equity in a company
- Real estate that produces income
- Licensing rights to intellectual property
- Tools, platforms, or channels that allow you to publish or sell without permission

Ownership signals independence.
You don't rely on being chosen. You move on your own terms.

2. Brand

Your brand is the **story people tell about you** when you're not in the room.
It's not just a logo or a personal website—it's your **reputation, consistency, and strategic presence.**

A strong brand:

- Speaks before you do
- Attracts aligned opportunities
- Allows you to **charge more, speak less, and be trusted faster**

And unlike a resume, your brand compounds.
Every piece of content, every interaction, every result you deliver stacks into perception—and perception creates pull.

---

3. Reputation

If brand is external, **reputation is relational.**

This is the **currency of trust.**
It determines whether you get invited into deals, introduced to power circles, or offered leverage others never see.

You build it by:

- Doing what you say you'll do
- Operating with integrity when no one's watching
- Overdelivering when you could get away with average

And once it's built, reputation becomes a magnet.
You stop chasing—you're remembered and referred.

Why this matters:

In a noisy world where most people are trying to *signal* wealth through consumption,
The truly powerful signal it through **structure.**

The rich don't need to tell you they're rich.
Their positioning does the talking.

A portfolio speaks louder than a car.
A track record commands more attention than a status post.
And a reputation backed by results is the strongest currency in any room.

These are the **symbols of power** that matter.
And unlike status symbols, they can't be faked.
They're not bought—they're built.

Ownership. Brand. Reputation.
Start there.
Because when these are in place, money follows—not out of luck, but out of design.

Building Assets from Energy and Action

If wealth is built on ownership, then the next question is:
What are you building that you actually own?

Most people spend their days working, performing, or reacting—but create nothing that endures beyond the moment.
They give energy… but they don't **store** it.
They act… but they don't **build** from it.

The wealthy do the opposite.
They turn effort into **assets.**
Every hour spent, every move made, becomes part of something that keeps paying them—whether through income, influence, or access.

Let's break this down.

What is an asset?

An asset is **anything that continues to deliver value—even after you've stopped actively working on it.**

These are just examples. What matters most is not the format—but that it **outlives your effort and returns value without demand.**

This could be:

- A digital course that sells while you sleep
- A YouTube video that generates leads years after upload
- A licensing deal that pays you for work you no longer do
- A rental property that earns income while you focus elsewhere

- A strong personal brand that attracts deals, invitations, and leverage
- An email list or community you own—your direct, permissionless channel
- A software tool or content library that solves problems without your presence
- A well-crafted offer, system, or product that scales without burnout

In short:
Assets are proof of leverage.
They turn action into infrastructure.

How do you build one?

You start with a core question:

How can I turn my energy into something that lasts, scales, or compounds?

Here's a simple framework:

1. Document, don't just do.
Turn your process, method, or insight into something teachable or repeatable.

If someone asked you how you get results—could you explain it clearly, or show it step-by-step?

2. Package, don't just perform.
Instead of 1:1 output, ask: *How can this value live independently of me?*

Could your solution be turned into a guide, course, product, or template others can use without you present?

3. License or scale, don't just share.
Build it once, but allow it to earn repeatedly—through sales, distribution, or syndication.

Where could this value be sold, shared, or syndicated—so it continues to return income, trust, or access?

This is how a single burst of inspired work can pay dividends for years.

From survival output to sovereign structure

When you're trapped in the survival loop, your energy is always reactive:

- You work to get paid
- You post to get seen
- You launch just to stay relevant

But when you start building assets, your energy becomes **strategic**:

- Every move adds to your ecosystem
- Your presence multiplies, even in absence
- You stop operating from pressure—and start operating from vision

Your energy is your most valuable currency.
But only if it's used to build what keeps giving back.

You don't need millions to start building wealth.
You need a shift—from temporary hustle to **permanent structure**.

Assets are how energy becomes sovereignty.
And sovereignty is the only real luxury worth chasing.

PART III — The Rise of the Sovereign

"You do not chase wealth—you become the one it follows."

This is where it all converges.
Not theory, not mindset, not strategy alone—**embodiment.**

Sovereignty is not about control over others.
It's about **self-governance**—the ability to direct your energy, your attention, and your resources in alignment with who you really are.

It's where wealth stops being something you chase…
And starts being something that responds to the **person you've become.**

This part of the Codex will show you:

- The power habits that structure a sovereign life
- How to build "wealth portals" that align money with mission
- How to hold power without collapse or sabotage
- And how to activate a personal system that works, long after motivation fades

The sovereign path is not louder.
It's **cleaner, sharper, more directed.**

Now, we begin that path—one aligned move at a time.

Chapter 8: Power Habits of Sovereignty

The rituals, patterns, and codes of the truly rich

You don't rise to the level of your goals.
You fall to the level of your **habits.**

Every day, whether you realize it or not, you're casting votes for the identity you're becoming.

And while the average person is reacting to life—notifications, bills, moods, demands—those who live in sovereignty don't just *have* habits.
They have **rituals.**
Patterns of power. Codes of alignment.

These aren't about perfection.
They're about **design**—structuring your energy, attention, and decisions to flow toward outcomes you've chosen on purpose.

The wealthy don't just work differently.
They **live on a different frequency**—because their daily system keeps them in alignment with power.

This chapter reveals those systems.
Not the hype.
The actual rhythms behind long-term expansion.

Wealth Alignment Through Daily Rhythm and Focus

Sovereignty isn't built in spurts of motivation.
It's constructed through **rhythm.**
Through the consistent, quiet choices that stack into power over time.

Every sovereign life runs on a set of aligned patterns:
How you start the day. What you give your attention to. When you create, and when you receive.
These patterns are not rigid—they're **deliberate.**

Because wealth is not random.
It flows where energy is focused and decisions are coherent.

Why rhythm matters more than routine

Anyone can wake up early.
Anyone can build a morning checklist or download a planner.

But sovereign rhythm isn't about discipline for discipline's sake.
It's about creating **internal alignment with external action.**

When your days are structured around your highest priorities:

- You stop leaking energy into distraction
- You reduce decision fatigue
- You enter creative flow more easily
- You gain momentum without burning out

Most people chase clarity.
But clarity comes from **repetition, reflection, and ritual.**

You don't think your way into alignment.
You *act* your way into it—by designing your day around what you say you want.

The sovereign's focus filter

Wealthy people don't just manage their time.
They manage their **focus bandwidth.**

Ask yourself:

- What deserves my attention today—not just what demands it?

- What would I still be doing if I were already wealthy?

- What am I avoiding that would multiply my momentum?

These questions aren't just for planning.
They're for **alignment.**

Every time you choose focus over frenzy, you're proving to yourself—and the world—that you are sovereign over your state.

Sovereignty is not a feeling.
It's a pattern.

It shows up in your calendar.
In your first hour of the day.
In what you say yes to—and what you refuse to give energy to anymore.

And once your days reflect your destiny, wealth doesn't have to be chased.
It's simply the echo of who you've become.

Morning Manifestation, Decision Priming, Energetic Hygiene

The first hour of your day holds disproportionate power.

It's not just when your brain is most impressionable.
It's when your identity is most **pliable**—before the world invades with noise, demands, and distraction.

The sovereign doesn't waste that hour.
They use it to **tune**—to align energy, prime decisions, and calibrate to the frequency of power.

Let's break that down.

Morning Manifestation: Creating Before Consuming

Most people wake up and check their phone.
They scroll. React. Absorb.
By the time they've had coffee, they're already inside someone else's narrative.

The sovereign wakes differently.
They **create first.** They connect inward, not outward.

This doesn't have to be mystical.
It can be as simple as:

- Journaling your next-level identity
- Visualizing key moves for the day
- Speaking a power statement or affirmation
- Writing down what you're creating, not what you're fearing

This isn't wishful thinking or vague positivity.
It's **identity reinforcement**—training your nervous system to expect what you've chosen.

You don't manifest by wishing.
You manifest by anchoring your attention on *what you are actively becoming*.

Decision Priming: Preloading Your Sovereignty

Your day is a cascade of choices.
But if you don't prime your decision filters in the morning, you'll default to emotion, urgency, or habit.

Start with:

- One big thing you will move forward today
- One thing you will say no to—even if it's easy
- One decision that reflects the version of you who already has what you want

Write these down. Speak them out loud.
You are **preloading your alignment**—so your later self doesn't have to scramble under pressure.

Energetic Hygiene: Guarding Your Frequency

You shower to clean your body.
But do you cleanse your attention?

Every piece of content you consume, every low-vibration conversation, every doom-scroll moment leaves a residue.

Energetic hygiene means:

- Setting clear inputs (what you watch, read, listen to)
- Creating buffer zones before and after deep work
- Starting the day with **intention, not intrusion**

This isn't about being hyper-productive.
It's about being *energetically sovereign*.

You don't owe your first hour to the algorithm.
You owe it to the version of you that's building something timeless.

The goal isn't a perfect morning.
It's a powerful one.

Because if you win your energy early, the rest of the day flows differently.
And that frequency shift—over time—builds the life your future self will thank you for.

Sacred Discipline and Chaos Resistance

If your power can be disrupted by every distraction, delay, or dopamine hit—then it's not power.
It's potential.

The sovereign path doesn't just require clarity.
It requires **fortification**—a form of discipline that isn't rigid or performative, but **sacred**.

This isn't about productivity for productivity's sake.
It's about protecting the frequency you've worked to build—especially when the world starts spinning.

Sacred discipline vs. survival discipline

Most people only act when pressured:
Deadlines, crises, fear of failure.

That's survival discipline—forced action to avoid collapse.

Sovereign discipline is different.
It's **chosen action in service of who you're becoming.**

You don't move because you're scared.
You move because you're committed.

That's the energy the wealthy operate from:
They create rhythm in chaos.
They build through uncertainty.
They stay grounded when others spiral.

And it's not because they're stronger.
It's because they've trained for resistance.

Chaos is a certainty—your rhythm is the shield

There will be noise.
There will be unexpected bills, emotional dips, market swings, sick days, tech glitches, slow months.

You don't control the chaos.
But you **do control the codex** you operate from when it hits.

Ask yourself:

- What's my non-negotiable action, even on low-energy days?
- What routines reconnect me to alignment when I get shaken?
- What do I trust—when motivation disappears?

Discipline is less about control and more about **returning.**
Returning to rhythm. Returning to intention. Returning to the work that builds your foundation.

Sovereignty isn't about never being knocked off course.
It's about returning faster, cleaner, and sharper each time.

Sacred discipline is what makes that possible.
Not for ego. Not for aesthetics.
But so you can **withstand uncertainty and still move forward.**

That's what makes you dangerous—in the best way.

Chapter 9: Creating Wealth Portals

Income that aligns with purpose and expansion

There's income that sustains.
There's income that drains.
And then there's **income that expands you**—spiritually, creatively, and financially.

This is a **wealth portal**:
A system, offering, or asset that channels your energy into value—then multiplies it in a way that's aligned with your deeper mission.

Wealth portals aren't just business models.
They're **vessels for becoming.**

The sovereign doesn't chase money.
They build structures that magnetize it—**not by force, but by frequency.**

This chapter shows you how to:

- Identify the path of income that matches your gifts
- Build systems that return wealth without draining your soul
- Multiply value in ways that support both **profit and purpose**

Because true freedom isn't just about having money.
It's about creating in a way that expands you while enriching others.

The Three Paths: Value Creation, Value Capture, Value Leverage

Wealth isn't mysterious.
It flows through three clear paths:
You **create value**, **capture value**, or **leverage value**.

Most people only focus on one—and usually the least scalable. The sovereign understands all three, and builds systems that move between them fluidly.

Let's break each one down:

---

1. Value Creation — The Generator

This is where it all begins.
You create something that didn't exist before—or do it better than anyone else.

It could be:

- A product, service, offer, or method
- A piece of content, insight, or solution
- A space, experience, or transformation

Creation is sacred.
But many creators get stuck here, because they think *creating = earning*.
It doesn't. Not automatically.

Creation starts the energy. But unless you structure how that value is received and returned, you're just giving—and depleting.

2. Value Capture — The Container

This is where most people struggle.

You might have amazing insight or work—but **have you structured a way to receive value in return?**

Examples:

- Turning free content into paid offers
- Having clear calls to action, price points, and purchase pathways
- Collecting and owning your data (emails, customer relationships, platforms you control)

If creation is fire, capture is the **furnace.**
It contains the energy so it becomes usable heat—not a flare-up that dies out.

Without capture, you're valuable but broke.
You give, inspire, post—but there's no container to **hold** the return.

---

3. Value Leverage — The Multiplier

This is where sovereignty scales.

You take the value you've created and captured—and build systems that **amplify** it.

This could be:

- Turning coaching into courses
- Turning a blog into a book
- Using media or automation to deliver your offer 24/7

- Turning one service into a licensing model or ecosystem

Leverage isn't laziness.
It's wisdom.

It says: *If this is good, let's make sure it reaches more people with less friction.*

This is how sovereigns escape the time-for-money trap.
They take something real—and let it echo through systems.

Why this matters:

If you only create, you burn out.
If you only capture, you stall.
If you only leverage without real value, you become noise.

But when you do all three—**in alignment**—you've built a portal.

Something that brings energy into the world, receives compensation in return, and expands beyond your personal bandwidth.

Creation starts the fire.
Capture contains it.
Leverage spreads the light.

This is how wealth becomes more than income.
It becomes *infrastructure for impact.*

Evergreens: Digital Assets, Systems, Capital

If you had to stop working tomorrow—what would keep earning for you?

That's the question most people avoid.
Because deep down, they know the answer is: **nothing.**

Their income is effort-dependent.
When the effort stops, the money stops.
Which means they don't own a business—they own a treadmill.

Sovereigns don't operate this way.
They build **evergreens**—assets, systems, and positions that keep returning value long after the initial work is done.

Let's break these down:

---

1. Digital Assets — Value That Outlives the Creator

Digital assets are anything you create once that can deliver results repeatedly:

- Courses, ebooks, trainings
- Templates, frameworks, toolkits
- Subscription content, memberships, or licensing deals
- Content libraries, video series, brand ecosystems

These can be sold, distributed, bundled, or repurposed.

They're not just products—they're **energy storage systems.**

They capture your best ideas, methods, or content and give them a life of their own.

If you stop creating tomorrow, your assets still speak, still teach, still earn.
That's evergreen power.

---

2. Systems — Infrastructure That Moves Without You

Systems aren't glamorous.
But they're what separates chaotic creators from **sovereign builders.**

Systems can be:

- A sales funnel that filters leads while you sleep
- An onboarding flow that turns strangers into loyal clients
- An SOP library that allows your team to execute without constant input
- A calendar rhythm that protects your focus and output

Systems don't just save time—they **multiply capacity.**

You're not making more decisions.
You're making fewer decisions that matter more.

And when your systems run, your energy is freed to **create, scale, or rest.**

---

3. Capital — Money That Builds More Money

Most people treat money as a tool for spending.

Sovereigns treat it as a **soldier.**

Every dollar is deployed with intention—to buy time, to build assets, or to seed investments that return more value.

Capital evergreen strategies might include:

- Investing in index funds, real estate, or scalable businesses
- Lending through peer-to-peer platforms or funding systems
- Equity stakes in ventures aligned with your vision
- Cash reserves that reduce reactivity and unlock long-term plays

Capital gives you breathing room.
Breathing room gives you power.

Why Evergreens Matter:

When your energy is tied to income, your nervous system is always in alert mode.
But when you have evergreens—your assets, systems, and capital move with or without you.

You stop needing to hustle.
You start choosing when and how you want to move.

And that's the point:
Freedom isn't the absence of work—it's the ability to direct your work toward what matters most.

Evergreens give you that power.

Examples of Wealth Portals Built by Alignment, Not Hustle

It's easy to talk about building aligned income.
But what does that actually look like?

Let's strip away the fluff and look at **real models**—not theoretical hype, but actual wealth portals built through a mix of skill, alignment, and sovereign design.

These are not meant to be copied.
They're here to **reveal the pattern**:
When energy is focused, value is structured, and systems are in place—wealth flows with *far less friction*.

---

1. The Mentor-Author

They spent years in a service business—consulting, coaching, guiding others one-on-one.
But burnout hit. They loved the work, hated the calendar.

So they built a portal:

- They turned their framework into a self-paced course
- They wrote a book that built credibility while they slept
- They launched a group cohort model with seasonal enrollment
- They licensed their process to other coaches for a percentage of revenue

From 100% time-for-money → to leveraged, evergreen value delivery.
Same mission. More scale. Less exhaustion.

2. The Creator-Teacher

They started with YouTube videos, sharing knowledge in a niche field.
No ads. No products. Just consistent value.

Over time:

- The content brought in leads, trust, and a growing community
- They launched a paid workshop, then bundled it into a digital course
- Built a newsletter, sold sponsorships, opened a private membership space
- Added affiliate income from tools they authentically use and love

Their portal is an ecosystem.
Every piece of content points toward a deeper relationship—and every asset reinforces the next.

No chasing. No hype. Just **compounding trust.**

3. The Artisan-Strategist

They had a craft—design, storytelling, branding.
What they didn't have was scale.

So instead of grinding through freelance projects forever, they:

- Created template packs that solved repeat client problems

- Built an agency with documented systems and a trained team

- Sold a "done-with-you" program that combined strategy + consulting

- Invested part of their earnings into a personal brand that opened consulting, teaching, and partnership doors

They didn't abandon their art.
They *structured it*.

Now their time goes toward creative growth—not survival output.

The Pattern is Sovereignty

In every case, it wasn't about going viral, chasing clients, or burning out.
It was about:

- **Clarifying their value**

- **Owning their method**

- **Building systems to deliver it at scale**

None of them started with perfect clarity.
They **built as they walked.**
They pivoted, refined, and aligned.

Wealth portals aren't found.
They're *crafted*.
And the more aligned you are—the more magnetized they become.

Chapter 10: The Inner Citadel

Keeping your power once you've built it

Not all losses are financial.
Some are internal.

Success can stretch you. Visibility can test you.
And abundance—if you're not grounded—can trigger every wound you thought you left behind.

That's why sovereign wealth isn't just about what you earn.
It's about what you can **hold** without collapse, sabotage, or self-erasure.

This chapter is about the citadel:
The inner structure that protects your power once it arrives.

You've dismantled illusions.
You've built systems.
Now you must guard the only thing that can truly lose it all—
yourself.

Here you'll learn:

- How to build spiritual resilience under pressure
- How to hold abundance without guilt, fear, or chaos
- How to live *from* wealth—not just in pursuit of it

Because if your external world grows faster than your inner capacity, the whole system shakes.
But if you fortify the citadel—you don't just keep the wealth.
You *become the wealth*.

Spiritual Resilience Under Pressure

Wealth doesn't just amplify your life.
It amplifies **you.**

Your beliefs. Your habits. Your shadows.
Whatever is unresolved will rise as you rise.

This is why so many people lose momentum after their first breakthrough:

- The income arrives—and triggers guilt.
- The visibility grows—and awakens imposter syndrome.
- The freedom expands—and reveals how uncomfortable peace can feel.

Without inner resilience, you don't hold more—you **leak more.**

The myth of "arriving"

Most people think their problems disappear with success.

But in reality, success:

- Increases responsibility
- Multiplies decisions
- Exposes unhealed narratives
- Demands deeper clarity

This doesn't mean success is a burden.
It means it's a **mirror.**

And you need a structure inside that can **see clearly without collapsing.**

What is spiritual resilience?

It's not about being unshakable.
It's about being **recenterable.**

Spiritual resilience means:

- You don't mistake pressure for punishment
- You can stay calm when energy spikes—good or bad
- You can return to clarity faster than chaos can claim you

You're not outsourcing peace to your results.
You're cultivating a **state that holds**—no matter what the bank account, launch metrics, or market says today.

Practices that strengthen your citadel:

Stillness
5–10 minutes of silence each day—not to force peace, but to **witness what's present** without judgment.
No music. No stimulation. Just you and your breath.

Stillness isn't absence.
It's listening—and it sharpens the space between reaction and choice.

With time, it builds inner spaciousness—the ability to hold intensity without flinching, and to act without reacting.

Your mind is not your master.
It's your instrument—but only if you know how to hear beyond it.

Check-ins with Truth

Truth is your internal compass. But it goes quiet under noise, pressure, or performance.

Pause daily or weekly and ask:

- "Am I acting from alignment or fear?"
- "Am I building from ego or service?"
- "What does the version of me who's already at peace choose here?"

They're **mirrors**—portals back to clarity.

They sharpen discernment, strip away emotional fog, and return you to the version of you that moves from center, not chaos.

And the more often you return, the faster the storm loses power.

Ritualized Resets

We don't drift into alignment—we **return to it.**

Set structured moments—weekly, monthly, quarterly—to:

- Review what you've built
- Realign your goals
- Reconnect with your *why*

Use journaling, long walks, sacred solitude, or intentional review practices.

These aren't luxuries. They're maintenance for your nervous system.

Because pressure that isn't processed becomes sabotage.

But pressure that is seen, felt, and honored—becomes power you can direct.

You don't build resilience in the moment you need it.
You build it **before**, so when the moment comes—you're ready.

You don't need to be perfect.
You need to be rooted.

And once you are, no win can unground you.
No loss can undo you.
Because your citadel stands—not as armor, but as **alignment made durable.**

How to Handle Abundance Without Self-Sabotage

You've been taught how to chase success.
But have you been taught how to **hold it**?

Abundance isn't just money in your account.
It's expansion—of possibility, visibility, and power.

And if you haven't prepared for that expansion internally, you'll unconsciously do what so many do:
Push it away. Burn it down. Or quietly shrink to feel safe again.

Self-sabotage doesn't always look like failure.
It often looks like "just taking a break," "simplifying," or "focusing on other things."
But beneath it, there's fear.

Why we fear abundance

Abundance challenges your identity.

It asks:

- *Can you receive without guilt?*
- *Can you own your voice without apology?*
- *Can you take up space without waiting for permission or validation?*

If your nervous system has been wired for survival, success can feel like a threat.
Not because it's bad—but because it's unfamiliar.

You don't sabotage because you're weak.
You sabotage because part of you doesn't feel **safe** with more.

The subtle forms of sabotage

- You procrastinate at the edge of a breakthrough
- You underprice your offers to stay likable
- You stop promoting right when things start working
- You ignore your systems and default to burnout
- You start drama to avoid peace
- You "accidentally" lose momentum after a big win

None of this means you're broken.
It means you've hit a threshold—and your inner blueprint doesn't match your outer growth.

How to expand your capacity to hold more

1. Normalize success
Repetition creates safety.
Review your wins weekly. Acknowledge your success out loud—not to impress others, but to anchor it in your own nervous system.
Not bragging. Just integration.
Let your system learn: *This is not a fluke. This is my new floor.*

2. Ground in purpose
Money without meaning feels empty—and emptiness triggers sabotage.
Anchor your growth to mission. Remind yourself why it matters—who or what you're doing it for.
It might be your mission. Your family. Your future self. Or simply the life you've chosen to live fully.

3. Let it be safe to be seen

Visibility brings up fear of judgment, rejection, failure.
But sovereignty means: *I do not shrink to make others comfortable.*
You are not dangerous because you shine.
You are dangerous when you pretend not to.

4. Create "wealth safety" rituals

Daily moments that anchor calm in the face of more:

- Breathwork before checking financials
- Gratitude journaling after receiving payments
- Declaring new standards instead of shrinking to old habits

The goal isn't to be fearless.
The goal is to **stay in motion even when fear rises.**

Abundance doesn't destroy you.
It reveals what parts of you still need to be claimed, cleared, and calibrated.

And once you do that work, success stops being a threat—and starts being **home.**

Living From Wealth, Not Chasing It

Wealth isn't just what you have.
It's how you move.

You can be rich and still live in scarcity.
You can have millions and still operate like you're one mistake from collapse.

The sovereign doesn't just *have* wealth.
They live *from it*.

This is the shift:
From chasing to embodying.
From earning to emanating.
From hustle to harmony.

Chasing is survival. Living is sovereign.

Most people—even after success—are still chasing:

- The next milestone
- The next launch
- The next external validation

Chasing comes from the belief that *something is still missing*.
That you must *reach* to be enough.

But when you begin to live from wealth, everything changes:

- Your decisions come from clarity, not urgency
- Your relationships come from overflow, not need
- Your creations come from joy, not pressure

You stop trying to "become" successful.
You simply operate as someone who already is.

Signs you're still chasing

- You say yes to opportunities that drain you—because you fear missing out
- You overwork to justify your success
- You under-celebrate to stay humble
- You shrink your truth to stay palatable
- You plan from lack, not from vision

This is not about judgment.
It's about awareness.

You don't have to wait for perfect conditions to stop chasing.
You just have to choose a new point of origin.

What it means to live *from* wealth

- You act from trust, not tension
- You create from conviction, not just trend.
- Your work is led by vision and values—not by algorithms.
- You rest without guilt
- You spend with purpose
- You hold with grace

This is where you stop seeing wealth as something **outside of you**…
And start treating it as a **state that flows through you.**

It's not passive. It's not delusional.
It's not "just believe and wait."

It's energetic authorship—combined with strategic action.
And it's the only way to build a life that doesn't just look wealthy—but feels free.

You've earned the right to stop running.
Now comes the embodiment.

You're not building wealth to finally feel whole.
You're building it from the wholeness you've already reclaimed.

Chapter 11: The Codex in Practice

Activating your personal wealth system

This book was never just about information.
It was a **transformation**—a deconstruction of illusion and a reconstruction of sovereign power.

You've seen the illusion.
You've learned the structure.
You've reclaimed your sovereignty.

Now it's time to **activate your own Codex.**

Not mine.
Not someone else's blueprint.
Yours.

Because true wealth isn't found in imitation.
It's built through **intention + alignment + action**—repeated over time, guided by your internal compass.

This chapter is your integration point.
A place to clarify your wealth system: how you think, what you build, and how you hold power without collapsing.

You don't need to master everything to begin.
You just need to choose your **starting alignment**—and build from there.

Let's walk through how.

Build-Your-Own Codex: Mindset + Mission + Method

You've absorbed the laws.
You've broken the illusions.
Now it's time to **build your own system**—one that aligns thought, purpose, and action into a personal engine of wealth.

This isn't about perfection.
It's about **precision.**

Every sovereign codex is built from three pillars:

---

1. Mindset — Your Inner Operating System

Your mindset isn't just what you believe.
It's the **lens you use to interpret the world.** It filters opportunities, threats, value, and worth.

Ask yourself:

- What are my new wealth beliefs—and how do I reinforce them daily?
- Where do I still hesitate to trust my capacity to receive, build, or lead?
- What emotional state is my most creative and clear—and how do I return to it?

You're not building wealth from survival anymore.
You're building it from **sovereign frequency.**

Lock in your core mindset rituals.
The world you experience will rise to match them.

2. Mission — Your Direction and Desire

This is the "why" behind everything you build.

It doesn't have to be world-changing.
It just has to be **aligned**—with your values, your energy, and your definition of success.

Ask yourself:

- What kind of life am I actually designing?
- Who do I want to become through the process of wealth-building?
- What kinds of problems do I feel lit up to solve—for myself and others?

Your mission doesn't need to be loud.
But you owe it to yourself to be honest about it—because only truth can fuel you when strategy isn't enough.

---

3. Method — Your Systems and Structures

This is where vision becomes infrastructure.

Ask yourself:

- What am I building that can grow without constant input?
- Where does my energy go—and how can I redirect it toward leverage?
- What's the first (or next) wealth portal I can focus on building?

Don't try to build ten things at once.
Focus. Systematize. Multiply.

Your method becomes your **engine**.
And when it's aligned with mindset and mission—you don't just grow wealth.
You **embody it.**

This is your codex:

- Your way of thinking
- Your way of serving
- Your way of building

Wealth is not a template.
It's a transmission powered by who you've chosen to become.

And now, you choose.
Not with pressure—but with clarity.

Bringing Your Codex to Life: Translate → Structure → Act

Insight alone doesn't transform lives.
Applied clarity does.

Now that you've defined your Codex—your mindset, mission, and method—it's time to translate those into a personal system that breathes in the real world.

This isn't about doing more.
It's about doing what matters, with consistency and conviction.

---

1. Translate Insight into Intention

Before strategy comes **sovereign choice.**

You've absorbed dozens of insights. Now filter them into a personal foundation you can stand on.

Ask yourself:

- What am I done tolerating—from myself, my environment, or my income sources?
- What season am I entering—and what kind of energy is required to lead it?
- What 1–3 personal wealth codes will guide how I think, build, and move from this point forward?

These "codes" are simple truths you choose to live by.
Examples:

- "I only build scalable income."
- "I never trade time for money without leverage."

- "I protect my energy like capital."
- "Money flows where I focus."
- "I build systems that free me."
- "I earn from alignment, not approval."

Write yours. Speak them. Repeat them until they become reflex. This is your new operating system. And sovereign systems don't run on default.

---

2. Structure One Path

You don't need ten portals. You need **one built with precision.**

Most people get stuck in idea overwhelm.
You're here to simplify, commit, and execute.

What is the single wealth portal I am committing to next?

Choose one clear vehicle that aligns with your energy, skills, and stage.
It could be:

- A product, service, or digital offer
- A brand asset (like a course, YouTube channel, or licensing play)
- A system that automates or scales what you already do
- A reinvestment strategy to turn earned income into passive capital flow

This is not "everything I want to build someday."
This is *the one portal* that gets your next 90 days of focused creation.

It doesn't have to be big.
It has to be **real**—and buildable with the skills, tools, or support you can reasonably access and activate.

What does "done" look like?

Define the finish line clearly:

- Is it **launched** and in the world?

- Is it **monetized** and bringing in leads or sales?

- Is it **automated** or scheduled to run without your constant input?

- Is it **repeatable**, with a system or process you can scale or delegate?

If it's vague, it won't get finished.
So make it binary: "Yes, it's done" or "No, it's not."

Done is not perfection.
Done is *functional, testable, and able to evolve.*

What are the 3–5 key actions I must complete to build this portal in the next 30–90 days?

Every vision needs a runway.
What gets you from idea to asset?

Break it down into **clear, finishable moves.** For example:

- Define the offer + outcomes
- Build the landing page or sales flow
- Design the delivery or automation system
- Record or produce key assets
- Set launch, pre-sell, or outreach plan
- Create a 3-email nurture sequence or onboarding flow

Then: put those actions on a **timeline**.

Sovereignty means your calendar reflects your codex—not your distractions.

You don't need complexity.
You need **clarity + commitment**—repeated until something is built that lasts.

---

3. Act in Rhythm, Not Reaction

You've clarified your focus. You've chosen your wealth portal.

Now you move.

Not someday. Not when you feel ready.
Now.

Because without movement, there is no integration.
There's only intention on pause—and pause becomes paralysis.

You don't need to hustle.
But you do need to **enter the rhythm of sovereign motion.**

This is the difference between those who read about wealth…
And those who build it.

Establish a Ritual Cadence

This is how you create momentum without burnout—through rhythm that aligns with your Codex, not external chaos.

Weekly: Track → Celebrate → Refine

- Review what you actually accomplished—not just what stayed on your to-do list
- Celebrate even small completions (this wires in self-trust)
- Remove friction—eliminate what's slowing you or stealing energy

This is your weekly reset. Light. Fast. Focused.

Monthly: Audit → Adjust → Recommit

- Identify what drained vs. what delivered
- Ask: Where did I act from power, and where did I revert to reaction?
- Recommit to your primary portal or system—cut distractions that crept back in

This is your sovereign pulse-check. Don't skip it.

Quarterly: Zoom Out → Realign → Redesign

- Reconnect with your mission: Is this still the path that feels most alive?
- Audit your ecosystem: Are your systems still supporting scale and sanity?
- Redesign or optimize based on truth—not ego, trend, or pressure

This is where vision and structure realign.

These are not corporate reviews.
They're your **alignment checkpoints.**
Skip them, and drift returns.

Ritual > Reaction

Most people act from urgency.
You now act from rhythm.

Write these dates into your calendar. Set reminders. Make it sacred.

This is how you prove—not to others, but to yourself—that your actions reflect your architecture.

Consistency beats intensity.
Clarity protects your energy.
Action builds identity.

This is how the Codex becomes not just something you understand…
But something you *live*.

Questions for Self-Clarity

Sovereignty begins with clarity.
Not the kind you borrow from others—but the kind you extract from within.

These questions aren't meant to overwhelm you.
They're meant to **reveal you.**
To strip away noise, obligation, and inherited beliefs—so you can build from truth, not trend.

Take your time. Return often. Let these questions become your mirrors—because who you are will evolve, and your answers will too.
Use them not just to reflect, but to **recode your direction each season.**

MINDSET

- Where do I still operate from fear, scarcity, or approval-seeking?
- What beliefs about money or power am I still carrying that no longer serve me?
- When I feel most expansive—what's present in my environment, focus, or energy?
- What would change if I trusted myself fully?

MISSION

- If I stopped pretending I didn't know, what do I actually want?
- What kind of value do I most love creating?

- What kind of people or problems light me up to serve?
- What does wealth mean to *me*—beyond the numbers?

METHOD

- What is the most aligned wealth portal I can commit to building right now?
- What does "enough" look like for me in this season—and how does that shape my plan?
- Where am I complicating what could be simplified?
- What structure would make execution easier, faster, or more energizing?

These aren't questions to fill your journal.
They're keys—to patterns, clarity, and momentum.

Return to them every quarter. Ask again. Listen again.
You're not chasing the same life—you're building the next one.

Integration: Living the Codex

This book gave you the tools.
Now, it's on you to use them.

You've identified what no longer serves you.
You've clarified what you actually want to build.
You've structured a system that aligns mindset, mission, and method.

Now it's time to put it into motion—and keep it there.

What to remember:

- You don't need more information. You need consistent execution.

- You don't need to do it all. You need to do what matters most—well.

- You don't need to prove anything. You need to stay aligned with your own direction.

Sovereignty means taking responsibility for your results, without shame or delay.
It means knowing what you're working toward—and cutting what doesn't serve that focus.

What to do next:

1. **Pick your portal.** One offer, product, system, or path. Start there.

2. **Codex your calendar.** Block time. Remove noise. Protect your rhythm.

3. **Move forward weekly.** Small wins, repeated consistently, change everything.

Don't let momentum die in overthinking.
Build something real—then refine it as you go.

This isn't about hype.
It's about doing the work that matters, on your terms.

The Codex is yours now.
And it only works if you do.

Final Words: A Thank You

If you made it here, thank you—for your attention, your time, and most of all, your willingness to think for yourself.

This book wasn't designed to give you every answer.
It was built to challenge what you've accepted, offer what's often hidden, and help you build a system that actually works—for you.

What you do next is what matters.

Not perfectly.
Not all at once.
But with consistency, clarity, and the kind of focus most people never choose to protect.

Wealth is not a mystery.
It's a structure—built from the inside out.

And now, you have everything you need to start building it.

Build it. Live it. Let the Codex prove itself.

www.ingramcontent.com/pod-product-compliance
Lightning Source LLC
Chambersburg PA
CBHW072157160426
43197CB00012B/2425